When the Handwriting on the Wall Is in
on the Wall Is in

When the Handwriting on the Wall Is in

brown crayon

SUSAN L. LENZKES

DEVOTIONS
FOR THE
HARRIED
HOMEMAKER

ZONDERVAN
PUBLISHING HOUSE

OF THE ZONDERVAN CORPORATION
GRAND RAPIDS, MICHIGAN 49506

WHEN THE HANDWRITING ON THE WALL IS IN BROWN CRAYON
Copyright © 1981 by Susan L. Lenzkes

Second printing October 1981

Edited by Lisa Bouma

Library of Congress Cataloging in Publication Data
Lenzkes, Susan L.
    When the handwriting on the wall is in brown crayon.
    1. Meditations. 2. Lenzkes, Susan L. I. Title.
BV4832.2.L45   242   81-5008
ISBN 0-310-43631-1   AACR2

Published in the United States of America

To Wilda Finefrock,
my dear mom,
who has always
encouraged me to write,
even though I
started my career on
her clean walls.

And to Herb,
Cathy, Jeff, and Matthew,
my daily sources of
material and
love.

Foreword

Sue Lenzkes peeks into my life. She sees what no one else *ever* sees. She writes,

> Stoop shouldered
> foot dragging
> sighing
> resignation
> is not
> trust!

Then just as I am about to take a secret guilt trip, she defines what real trust is and turns my whole heart to the magnificence of exactly *who* it is I trust. What writing!

Most of us write fairly well out of past events, hindsight, and lessons learned well. But what touches this writer's heart is that Sue writes in the midst—the very midst—of life, husband, and kids as it's happening!

No wonder her writings are real, fresh, hope-filled, and practical. . . . She's one of us!

JOYCE LANDORF

Acknowledgments

Scripture quotations are from the King James Version unless otherwise indicated. The following versions of the Bible are also quoted:

LB   —The Living Bible, copyright © 1971 by Tyndale House Publishers.

MLB   —The Modern Language Bible, copyright © 1969 by Zondervan Publishing House.

NIV   —The Holy Bible: The New International Version, copyright © 1978 by the New York International Bible Society.

PHILLIPS —The New Testament in Modern English, translated by J. B. Phillips, copyright © 1958 by J. B. Phillips.

RSV   —The Revised Standard Version of the Bible, copyright © 1971 by the Division of Christian Education of the National Council of Churches of Christ in the United States of America.

Grateful acknowledgment is expressed to the following publishers for permission to quote the author's previously published works:

Tyndale House Publishers, Wheaton, Illinois, for the poems "Wasting the Present," "Discord," "High Expectations," and "Exercise in Love."

Christian Life Publications, Wheaton, Illinois, for the poems "Important Circles" and "Timely Appreciation."

An expanded version of the poem "Repair Work" has been illustrated and published by Ruth E. Westermann Bosch as a memorial to her four-year-old niece and six-year-old nephew who died in tragic circumstances, along with both parents, during the preparation of this book.

When the Handwriting on the Wall Is in

brown crayon

*Suddenly the fingers
of a human hand
appeared and wrote
on the plaster
of the wall.*

(Dan. 5:5 NIV)

Crayon Messages

When a message from God
would clear up confusion,
He could write on my wall—
or give the illusion.
But the writing that's there,
it's plain to be seen,
is a simple crayon drawing
that I've yet to clean.

Lord, help me to learn
I won't be receiving
a miraculous sign
wrought through believing;
when each day I can see
and yet don't apply
Your messages looking me
straight in the eye.

I live in a home with three levels of fingerprints. Our house often has happy faces grinning from the bathroom mirrors and wadded-up washcloths in the tub. It's a house with bedrooms accustomed to popped balloons, banana peels, and dirty socks for decor— plus a treasure map drawn in brown crayon on the wall above the boys' bed.

My kitchen has a counter that frequently seems to hold more used glasses than we ever owned, and a garbage disposal that regularly gobbles dishcloths, potscrubbers, and teaspoons. We sometimes refrigerate empty peanut butter and jam jars, and nobody ever knows who drank the last of the milk.

On occasion our home has broken dishes and broken bones, fears, squabbles, and tears. Other times it has hearty laughter and helping hands, surprises, accomplishments, and hugs.

And somehow, through it all, God has opened my eyes to His messages buried in each cluttered day: communiqués of love, words of wisdom, bulletins of understanding, signs of growth, and telegrams of truth.

Such messages are as likely to be found in the erratic scribbling of a day when everything is going wrong, as in the flowing script of that occasional day that's going my way.

But that's what makes life as God's child so fascinating. I never know when I'm going to scrub crayon markings off the wall and find an underlying meaning.

Today, for instance, I finally got around to scrubbing that treasure map off the boys' wall. As I pushed my soapy sponge from X to X, I could see more than crayon marks disappearing. Each vanishing X seemed to represent one short year after another—all the time God has given us to map out His truths in the lives of our children—the time we're allotted to help them find the treasure of a vital relationship with Jesus.

Establish our priorities, Lord.

He who guards his mouth
preserves his life:
he who opens wide his lips
comes to ruin.

(Prov. 13:3 RSV)

That's a Mouthful!

Don't look now, Lord!
I don't want You
to see me
standing here with
my big foot
crammed in my mouth.

Don't worry, child.
If I didn't love you
just as much with your
foot in your mouth,
I'd hardly ever get a
chance to love you.

Mothers are often forced to utter things other people wouldn't even think. One day I actually heard myself yelling in my hands-on-hips tone of voice, "All right! Who put the fire truck in the toilet?" I'll always wonder if there was a Fuller Brush man about to ring my doorbell who forever imagines our bathroom with a garage-sized commode.

A lot of motherly queries seem to be preceded by the weary words, "Who put the . . . ," and end with a scramble of objects so strange they could be a mad Parker Brothers' game of chance.

Over the years, anyone who happened to be in the wrong place at the right time could have heard me asking who put: the cereal behind the couch? (the ants found it first); the pine cones in my purse? (I discovered them during church); the lemon pudding mix in the wading pool? (it was gelling in the corners); the toothpaste on the wall? (it looked like a fluoridated Picasso); the toy dish in the oven? (the flames were leaping out the vent); and the potato peelings down the drain? (the bathtub drain)!

Actually, parents should be taught not to ask questions, because either no one did it, or the other guy did it. And if you ever do manage to pin the culprit, you tend to ask why. "*Why* did you put the rock in the refrigerator?" And then you get an answer: "Because I wanted a cold rock."

It's obvious that parenthood requires carloads of patience. And I could feel reasonably righteous about boisterously losing that patience when the going gets rough, if it weren't for the fact that God has to lavish so much of it on me.

Occasionally, after I've lost my temper at the children, I've heard my heavenly Father patiently asking, "Who put the foot in the mouth?"

13

*"Blessed are those
who hunger and thirst
for righteousness
for they shall be satisfied."*

(Matt. 5:6 RSV)

*The soul of the sluggard
craves and gets nothing,
while the soul of the diligent
is richly supplied.*

(Prov. 13:4 RSV)

Malnutritioned

Forgive us, Lord,
for snacking at Your feast,
nibbling at righteousness,
picking at Your promises,
and showing up at Your table
when we have time.

If we, Your own,
are undernourished by choice,
how can we expect to
feed a lost and hungry world?

It's one of those hollow days—the kind that finds me tugging at the refrigerator door and then wondering why. When I look inside, nothing looks good, not last night's leftover roast beef, or even that marvelous imported cheese. Yet I am hungry for something. So I eat and find I'm not satisfied.

Perhaps this means I'm starving spiritually. That must be it. I need to get alone and open my emptiness to God's fullness.

As I wait hungrily before the Lord on my knees, an interruption slowly opens the bedroom door. "Oh, no. Not one of my kids, Lord. Not now when I'm about to hear from You. Send him away, Jesus, so You can speak to me."

Quietly my little one stands beside me as I kneel, praying he'll leave, pretending I don't know. Silently he climbs onto my back, pounding me with his heartbeat, breathing softly into my hair.

Finally he whispers close to my ear, "Mommy."

"What?"

"Mommy, I'm hungry. Can I have something to eat?"

"Yes, honey. I'm coming. It's almost dinnertime."

And I rise from my knees, knowing my interruption is my answer, knowing God feels me clinging to Him as I wait to be filled—knowing it's almost dinnertime.

Jesus told his disciples:
"There was a rich man
whose manager was accused
of wasting his possessions.
So he called him in and asked him,
'What is this I hear about you?
Give an account of your management,
because you cannot be
manager any longer.'"

(Luke 16:1–2 NIV)

Wasting the Present

Forgive me, Father.
You gave me the
perfect gift of
right now,
and I threw it away
hoping for a
better gift
later.

Wastepaper cans are usually no topic for discussion—unless it's whose turn it is to empty them. But this morning as I contemplated our bedroom wastebasket, trying to decide which child to blame for its unrelieved condition, I noticed its contents.

It was just the usual trash: cast-offs and remains, leftovers from our living. Wrappers and tissue, scrap paper and four-ounce cups, paper tubes from inside toilet paper rolls and empty bottles that held shampoo and cosmetics, odds and ends, bits and pieces.

The ease of modern living creates a lot of refuse. And we're used to it. After all, there's always more where that came from. Someday the resources will run out, and the memory of our bloated trash cans will haunt us.

When my time on earth is running out, I wonder if the rubbish cans of my wasted moments will loom before me—minutes and hours casually discarded because there seemed to be an endless supply. I wonder who'll be waiting to empty the trash cans then.

So faith, hope, love abide,
these three;
but the greatest of these
is love.
(1 Cor. 13:13 RSV)

Parenthood

I searched—
but there definitely was *not*
a packet of instructions
attached to my children
when they arrived.
And none has since
landed in my mailbox.
Lord, show me how
to be a good parent.
Teach me to
correct without crushing,
help without hanging on,
listen without laughing,
surround without smothering,
and love without limit—
the way You love me.

Though I lecture and harp at my children and have not love, I will be background noise to rebellious thoughts.

And though I wisely warn them not to use the street as a playground, or they'll be killed; and though I patiently explain why snails live in mobile homes, and I give endless answers to life's other mysteries; and though I have faith that can remove mountains of ignorance—yet never hug my children—I have taught nothing.

And though I slave over a steaming stove with balanced diets and complicated recipes and even burn my fingers—yet never smile as I serve—I have not really fed them.

A truly loving mother suffers through unfinished sentences, clutter, nicks on furniture, sleepless nights, and adolescent insults, and is kind enough to think her kids are the greatest. A loving mother tries not to resent her children for being free like she used to be, and she doesn't brag about how *she* never talked to *her* mom that way.

Real love: considers a childish nightmare more urgent than her need for sleep; is not shattered by the title "Meanest Mom"; doesn't shame a toddler who breaks training or a teen who still spills milk; steadfastly refuses to entertain visions of escape; and does not smirk as her child trips over the toy he refused to put away (but with silent wisdom rejoices in the effective lessons of experience).

Mother-love has arms strong from lifting, a heart large with believing, a mind stretched with hoping, shoulders soft with enduring, and knees bent with committing.

True mother-love never fails to point her child to the Author of Love.

If it seem slow,
wait for it;
it will surely come,
it will not delay.
(Hab. 2:3 RSV)

Pacing

When I have to wait, God,
or when You want me to move slowly,
I don't like it.
I don't know which is worse,
staying in my shell
or coming out and crawling
at a snail's pace.
Make me content to do
whatever seems good to
You, Lord.
Your pace spells peace.

The doctor's office is not my favorite spot to spend a sunny spring morning. But that's exactly where I spent this one. It helped, though, that there was a sunny-faced little boy to watch. This blond, wide-eyed pre-schooler completely captivated me and everyone else with his eagerness to experience everything a doctor's waiting room could possibly offer.

He checked out the chairs and their occupants. He covered his baby sister with her checked blanket and tenderly explained that there was no need to be afraid. He marched down the hall to explore the bathroom, and a roomful of weary patients' eyes lit with amusement as his giggle echoed from behind the door. Perhaps he'd discovered he was finally tall enough.

He strutted back down the hall, arms swinging, and found a door that needed to be tested a few times. Magazines had to be straightened, and the holder for his sister's infant seat needed lowering. He carried on an effervescent conversation with a warm-hearted old man about the horror of shots and what it takes to be brave, his small round face registering complicated expressions with intensity.

Eventually, when he'd exhausted the room's possibilities, he announced with finality, "I'm tired of this place now. Let's go, Mommy."

"We have to wait, honey," she said.

"But I'm ready to go. Let's get out of here!"

He didn't really understand that he was waiting there for a purpose, his good health. He'd been so busy exploring the waiting room that he began to think that that was his purpose there. His inventive preoccupations finished, he felt he should move on.

Lord, sometimes You put me in Your waiting rooms. Help me to be patient with Your schedule. I need to learn all I can from those waiting rooms, but I should never forget that I must remain there until I see You. It's absolutely essential to my health.

And the ransomed
of the Lord shall return,
and come to Zion
with songs and everlasting joy
upon their heads:
they shall obtain joy and gladness,   .
and sorrow and sighing
shall flee away.
(Isa. 35:10)

Sing to him a new song.
(Ps. 33:3 NIV)

Discord

God,
when there's not
harmony between us,
remind me that
You
are always on the
right note.

Discouragement has landed. Vaguely I wonder why I'm discontent and feeling frustrated. After all, a Christian should be happy. I know, because 1 Thessalonians 5:16 says, simply and plainly, "Rejoice always." So a thick layer of guilt adds its weight to my discontent.

Sadly I sweep the same floor; wearily I wash the same dishes. And now I see it's time to repeat that familiar lecture. For here's my daughter, shaking her flute at me saying, "My teacher had better not give me this same song again. I'm sick of it! Seems like I've been playing it for the last hundred years!"

"My dear child, you're going to be on that song forever unless you learn to play it right. Stop trying to do it your way. Play it the way the composer wrote it, sounding each note correctly and surely. Then you'll begin to enjoy it. You'll be growing and learning—moving on to new lessons."

God poked me. "Listen to what you just said. Now give that lecture again, but to you from Me, the composer of your song. Play your song My way and you'll be happy again."

Blessed is the man
*who trusts in the L*ORD*,*
*whose trust is the L*ORD*.*
(Jer. 17:7 RSV)

*For thou art my hope, O Lord G*OD*:*
Thou art my trust from my youth.
(Ps. 71:5)

Trust

Stoop-shouldered,
foot-dragging,
sighing
resignation
is not trust.

Real trust
bounces on eager toes of
anticipation—
laughs with the pure delight
of knowing
in whom it believes—
rests easy
knowing
on whom it waits.

Lord,
so wrap me in the
knowledge of You
that my trust is no longer
in You, but
is You.

24

Children are cutest when no one's watching—or they think no one is.

I had just stepped into the kitchen with an armload of wash when the sight of our boys standing together on the back step caught my eye. Their backs were turned, so they didn't see me looking as the little one wrapped his arm around his brother's knees and tilted his blond head back, gazing up. He barely reached his brother's belt loops.

In a tiny voice he said, "Bend your ear down a minute—I want to tell you a secret."

Then, very quietly, he whispered something that delighted them both.

You know, Jesus, I can't help thinking as I watch them . . . after all these years of walking with You, I still don't even stretch to Your knees. Bend Your ear down a minute, I want to tell You a secret. I think You're wonderful. And I really do trust You. When I grow up I want to be just like You.

*"In just a little while
I will be gone from the world,
but I will still be
present with you.
For I will live again—
and you will too.
When I come back to life again,
you will know that I am in my Father,
and you in me, and I in you."*

(John 14:19–20 LB)

The Touch of God

Jesus,
I long to see You
face to face.
But for now
I love the way You
smile at me through
the face of a sister,
touch me with the
hand of a child,
speak to me through
the voice of a brother,
care for me with the
heart of a friend.

I was at the drinking fountain, swallowing aspirin and complaining to my friend about my frequent headaches.

She turned, put her arms around me, gave me a kiss, and then simply said, "I love you."

Warm surprise told me I must have expected a sermonette on searching for causes, a dissertation on slowing down, a checklist of ten things for which to be thankful, or at the very least, "My, that's too bad," followed by a hasty exit.

I guess I always expect You to preach at me, too, Jesus. Oh, how I wish You were *so real* that You could put Your arms around me and dissolve my petty complaints with "I love you."

"My child, I can. I did. At the drinking fountain."

Today, Lord, You gifted me with love, wrapped in a warm hug. Maybe I can pass it on to somebody else with a headache, or a heartache.

*"And in praying
do not heap up empty phrases
as the Gentiles do;
for they think that
they will be heard
for their many words."*

(Matt. 6:7 RSV)

Saying Surrender

Lord, I've heard people say,
"Give God your wallet
    and He'll have you."
You have my wallet, God.
That's easy—
it's usually empty anyway.
So how do I begin
to give myself completely?
"Give me your mouth, child.
    It's never empty.
    Then I'll have you!"

Sometimes I'm capable of impressing myself with my praying. Oh, not in public. But certainly in private.

The other morning I said, "Lord, help me to abide in the sunshine of Your love today, that I may radiate Your warmth to the world." Not only was God unimpressed with my words, but it rained all day.

Perhaps I should simply have said, "Lord, I never have trouble loving people when everything's going my way. Today will You help me to be willing to love when nobody seems to deserve it?"

I *am* learning to pray with the humility of true honesty. Yet even when I forget and start praying in lofty generalities, God pulls me up short by replying in specifics.

Not too long ago I blurted out, "Dear Jesus, I love You! More than pleasure, more than fame, more than approval, more than security, more than pride, even more than life!"

"More than pleasure?" He asked. "Then perhaps tonight you'll serve that extra piece of pie to someone else. More than fame? Maybe soon you'll write a great poem and forget to sign your name. More than approval? Then given another chance, you'll care more about your drop-in guests than your cluttered living room.

"More than security? Perhaps you'll trust Me for sufficient funds and still tithe. More than pride? Next time you'll fall flat and consider it a good position for prayer.

"More than life? I really loved *you* more than life."

For the wages of sin is death,
but the free gift of God
is eternal life
in Christ Jesus our Lord.

(Rom. 6:23 RSV)

Drink Ye All of It

Jesus, it was love
that forced Your trembling hand
to keep lifting, and Your
parched lips to keep drinking
the bitter cup of our salvation.
This was no toast to our health.
You raised the cup
alone in a dark garden,
sweating blood,
crying out for some other way—
yet obediently tilting it
higher, swallowing acid sin in
agonizing gulps.
You drank for Your friends
asleep nearby
and for Your enemies
converging with angry swords and
a cross.
You drank for us all and
drained the cup dry—
a pledge to eternal life.

I will remember, Lord. Eternally.

It's spring and time to paint the house. I knew it was hopeless to ask, but I asked anyway. "Please, honey, could we just leave the ivy twining so beautifully over the trellis porch? It would be easier for you. You wouldn't have to paint that part. After all, no one would know except us. It's hidden."

But just as I thought, he insisted, "We'll rip it down—it must be done right."

I couldn't believe it. That ivy with its lovely profusion of green glossy leaves was hiding massive snarled twisted limbs—limbs that started with slender tentacles small enough to slide between supporting beams, had then slowly, insidiously, almost imperceptibly expanded, wrenching our house apart at the seams!

I stood looking at the damage and suddenly knew what sin is like, seeming innocent, so small at first. But it grows, slowly, insidiously, leafed over with deceptive loveliness, until finally we're torn apart, destroyed.

No wonder it took such a drastic clean-up as Christ's death on the cross to prepare us for an eternity with God.

Thank You, Jesus, for the costly gift of salvation.

*She watches carefully
all that goes on
throughout her household
and is never lazy.
Her children stand
and bless her;
so does her husband.*

(Prov. 31:27–28 LB)

Important Circles

Lord, sometimes I resent
being like a clock
going round in circles
hour after hour,
all day long,
week after week,
doing the same thing.

Help me to remember how
everyone in this house
looks up to that clock
every few minutes
all day long,
week after week.

I remember the day I wrote my list of helpful hints for harried mothers. It was the same day I considered calling a designer/contractor to see about having a new kitchen floor installed—one fashioned after those ashtrays that whirl clean when you press a center button. Toys, spills, dirt, clutter, even kids—gone. At the touch of a button.

It was the day I soothingly calmed myself with the rationale that the more dishes I broke, the fewer there were to wash—the day I decided to tell everyone the real color of our carpet was mud brown, and the sun had simply faded the edges to avocado green.

It was that same day that I hit upon the genius of stuffing both my toddler's legs into one pantleg so that he could no longer outrun me.

No question about it—motherhood *does* seem to be a thankless vortex some days. Yet I need to realize that mothers run in highly important circles. It's easier to understand that truth when I remember that God trusted His only Son to the care of a mother.

But the fruit of the Spirit
is love, joy, peace,
patience, kindness, goodness,
faithfulness, gentleness, self-control;
against such there is no law. . . .
If we live by the Spirit,
let us also walk
by the Spirit.

(Gal. 5:22–23, 25 RSV)

Harvesting

As I examine the
vine of my life,
checking the growth,
I'm forced to admit
that the
Fruit of the Spirit
doesn't include
crab apples.

This morning as I sat at the breakfast bar drinking coffee and staring through sleepy eyes, I noticed our son's fish crowding to my side of their bowl gaping back at me. Most of the fish stared with a wide-eyed innocence, if not a downright friendly curiosity.

But there's one crabby fish in that bowl. Oh, he *looks* beautiful—a sleek smoke color with a stunning silver belly. It's on his face that the real fruit of his personality blooms.

His unblinking eyes swivel here and there, with a searching critical stare. And the black-ringed mouth between those glaring eyes not only turns petulantly down at the corners—it openly pouts. It constantly moves in a gripe, gripe, gripe motion. The other fish work their mouths too, but somehow theirs seem more a gentle kissing motion.

I wonder who's observing me, the look in my eyes and the shape of my mouth? I wonder if I kiss my world with God's love often enough?

For God is not
a God of confusion
but of peace.
(1 Cor. 14:33 RSV*)*

Right On

Right is right
and wrong is wrong
except, of course, when
right seems wrong
and wrong seems right.
But that means
right which seems wrong
was not right,
but wrong to begin with,
or else it is
delusion and therefore
still right. And
wrong that seems right
was not wrong,
but right to begin with,
or else it is
rationalization and therefore
still wrong. So
once you've determined
what is right and
what is wrong,
right is indeed right and
wrong is indeed wrong.
Right?

Our youngest child's preschool teacher met me at her classroom door with one hand steering my boy and the other partially covering a smile. As our little student bolted to the sidewalk she said with undisguised amusement, "I just witnessed a four-year-old theological discussion. I'd say your son won—at least he was pretty sure of himself."

At my puzzled expression, she explained that my boy had firmly announced to his friend over the morning snack that "God *flowered* Jesus."

Not stopping to question the feasibility of such an unusual statement, his friend simply took the opposing viewpoint and loudly retorted that in no way did God do such a thing.

"Oh, yes He did. I *know!*" protested our scholar. "It says in the Bible that God aRose Jesus!"

I wonder how often God smiles, or laughs out loud at our limited understanding of His great truths? I wonder how often we spread our misunderstanding between thick slices of rationalization and determination and force-feed it to others?

We can find peace in the knowledge that God knows, and someday so shall we.

Look after each other
so that not one of you
will fail to find
God's best blessings.
Watch out that no bitterness
takes root among you,
for as it springs up
it causes deep trouble,
hurting many
in their spiritual lives.

(Heb. 12:15 LB)

Dear God,
I have a problem.
It's me.

Dear Child,
I have an answer.
It's Me.

Bluejeaned and barefoot, I stood watering the flowers we planted in the place the ivy used to grow—that ivy my husband tore down when he was painting last summer.

As I drenched the blossoms of bright yellow, crimson, and white, I noticed again those green sprouts of ivy breaking defiantly through the ground. They were unwanted weeds disturbing the flowers. I'd had to snap them off several times before, and now it needed to be done again. The suspicion grew that I was feeding a chronic problem.

I guess the trouble stems from the fact that we left just a couple of roots in the ground. They were so big and had twisted themselves, snakelike, beneath the cement of our house's foundation, making it seem impossible to remove them.

I wonder if that's why I keep sprouting problems? Perhaps I harbored just a couple of roots of sin beneath the foundation when I tore down my old life, surrendering to God and His new plans. Now they're growing and interfering with the budding plants. I think I need to call in a Professional.

You do whatever is necessary to fix things, Lord. After all, my life is Your garden.

Thou preparest a table
before me
in the presence of mine enemies.
(Ps. 23:5)

On the Run

You've
prepared a table for
me, Lord?
A full-course
sit-down meal?
How lovely!
You know I'd enjoy that
but right now I *am*
on the run.
So much to do and
so little time to do it!
I'll grab something later—
maybe at the little
drive-thru down the road.

You *do* own the
franchise on all those
fast-food places . . .
don't You, Lord?

If someone slapped a $1.69 general-merchandise sticker on me today, it would somehow feel just right. It's one of those all-too-frequent days when I'm on everybody's resource shelf.

My husband needs a button on his shirt, help finding his keys, and dinner an hour early; the kids need an arbitrator, a chauffeur, a nurse, an in-house garbage collector, and their P.E. clothes washed immediately.

The PTA needs me at a meeting tonight, if I care about the quality of my children's education; the Heart Association needs a volunteer, if I have a heart; the polls need my vote, if I want to remain in a free country; my Sunday school class needs a social chairman, if I don't mind; my friend needs a babysitter, if I have time; my kitchen floor needs a mop, if I believe in the power of bacteria; and my Bible needs a dusting, if I believe in the power of God.

Maybe I should just run through the 23rd Psalm, since I'm in such a rush. It's so familiar—it shouldn't take long.

One thing though, Lord. Why does it say You prepare a table for me "in the presence of my enemies"? I don't have any *enemies* . . .

And she brought forth
her firstborn son,
and wrapped him in swaddling clothes,
and laid him in a manger;
because there was no room
for them in the inn.

(Luke 2:7)

Celebrating

What have we done to Your
birthday, Lord?
You came in the dark silence of
night, with softly muffled
stable sounds.
We "remember" with
stereos on high volume,
jingling bells, and loud parties.
You came to us surrounded by brown—
animals, dirt floor, straw, and
wooden manger.
We "remember" with
brilliant reds, greens, and
glittery tinsel.
With our sounds and colors of
celebration, do we truly
remember,
or simply
refashion
and thus reduce the glory?

Glancing at the lighted plastic face of the Santa decoration, as I was about to pull the plug on him and drag myself to bed, I had the urge to flatten his jolly dimples with my fist. It's not jolly old St. Nick on Christmas Eve, making his famous round-the-world trip in twelve hours. It's tired old Mom on Christmas Eve feeling like she circled the world, and not remembering why.

Shopping. Baking. Decorating. Corresponding. Wrapping. Entertaining. I'd been so busy making things perfect that I'd made a perfect mess of things. I suspected as much when I heard myself saying, "No, you can't have a gingerbread man. You'll get crumbs on my clean floor!" And again when my daughter asked for advice on her gift list and got instead a tiresome list of my endless duties.

But I knew for sure I'd scrambled life when my youngest called from the other room, "Mommy, are you going to be in a good mood on Christmas?"

There was an exhausted mother that first Christmas morning, too. She was weary, not from parties and shopping and baking and trimming, but from giving birth to the Son of God, the One who came to us in simplicity so that we could learn that glory doesn't need decorating, the One who came to bring us peace.

"Mommy?"

"Are you still awake?"

"Merry Christmas, Mommy."

And God is able to provide you
with every blessing in abundance,
so that you may always
have enough of everything
and may provide in abundance
for every good work.

(2 Cor. 9:8 RSV)

Across the Ocean

The echoing sound of
hollow stomachs, empty souls,
barely reaches me.
I'm in an important
church budget meeting.

The cry of
motherless babies, godless people,
scarcely moves me.
We're planning programs
for an exciting year.

The desperate scratching
of ragged fingernails on closed doors
hardly bothers me.
We have urgent
matters to discuss.

How dare these people
try to disturb us.
Don't they care
that we have to
pave the parking lot
this year?

The Missions Board was looking for a "hunger volunteer." I glanced down, decided it couldn't hurt, and agreed to the experiment. *It wouldn't injure me,* I told myself, *to feel for a couple of days the way half the world feels all the time. Maybe then I'd care more, pray more, give more.*

The first morning I skipped breakfast, cleaned house, and felt great. I drank a glass of water and thought how we all eat more often than is really necessary. I skipped lunch and my peripheral vision picked up the refrigerator as I drank my water. After twenty hours, water truly lost its appeal. As I stir-fried savory scents of spicy beef and bell peppers with onions I said, "I think I'll have a big tall juicy glass of . . . water."

Now when your body requests beef and you give it water, it retaliates with its gagging reflex. When your nose sniffs rolls baking and you say, "Tough. Have a glass of water," it pays you back by being ten times keener than usual. As I wrote to take my mind off food, even my fat dictionary began to smell tasty!

By the next evening I was becoming aware that my nerves were raw with hunger. So I valiantly called forth extra reserves of patience and humor for a scene of emotional trauma with our teenager. Somehow, it took me three times longer than usual to break through the misunderstandings. And when our boys pulled their usual bedtime stalling routine, I felt I was simply being righteously firm, but my eight-year-old said, "You've never been this mean before, Mommy."

The next morning I awoke with a stomach ache and a headache. As I fried the kids' eggs and buttered their toast, I honestly didn't want any. But my shaking hands said, "Eat!" so I did. And the shaking stopped.

What the rest of the world would give for a chance to make hunger a choice. I thank God for the privilege of giving until it hurts—I discovered that it hurts less than hunger.

Now the serpent was more crafty
than any of the wild animals
the Lord God had made.
He said to the woman,
"Did God really say
'You must not eat
from any tree in the garden'?"
(Gen. 3:1 NIV)

Inchworm

Inchworm, inchworm,
what are you measuring—
an inch worth of sin
to be had for the pleasuring?

Inchworm, inchworm,
do you not know—
an inch worth of sin
can do nothing but grow?

Inchworm, inchworm,
though you're updated—
I suspect the Old Serpent
and you are related.

Suddenly shrieks echoed from the garage of our new home. "Help, Dad! It's a snake—I think it's a rattler! Help, I can't get out. The garage door's locked!"

Telling me to stay put (he could have saved the time, I wasn't about to move), my husband rushed to our daughter's rescue, unlocking the door, reassuring her that "there are no rattlesnakes in our area."

Freed, she bolted inside to the safety of her room while I waited, trusting the Lord and my brave husband —in that order, because I don't trust *snakes* at all.

"Did you kill it?" I asked as he stepped inside. "Was it a rattler?"

"Naw, it was only a baby. I just scooted it into a grocery bag with a stick and gave it to the boys to show their friend across the street."

My eyes widened. "You gave them a *snake*? What if it really *is* a rattler?"

"Come on now," he soothed. "Stop worrying. I didn't see any rattles. Anyway, it was just a baby."

I followed him into calmer conversational waters, until we heard a commotion outside. The father of our son's friend was standing in the middle of our cul-de-sac shouting at neighbors to stand back as he brought his shovel down repeatedly on the head of our boys' new "pet." One peek in the bag was all their experienced eyes had needed. Apparently the canyons grow not only sagebrush, but rattlesnakes, too.

"We didn't know," I muttered humbly to our neighbor as we huddled our children near us. "Fortunately it was only a baby."

"Oh, they're just as poisonous. Maybe worse," she said matter-of-factly. "They strike, but haven't learned to release, so they just keep pumping venom."

Is there a small sin less deadly than that little rattlesnake, Lord? Do I sometimes take sin's power lightly, forgetting that baby sins have for their father the Old Serpent?

47

Fix your thoughts
on what is true
and good and right.
Think about things
that are pure and lovely,
and dwell on the fine, good things
in others. Think about
all you can praise God for
and be glad about.

(Phil. 4:8 LB)

Sands of Time

Lord, these incidents were
really just small irritating
pebbles
on the sandy beach of
my life.
So why did I magnify them?
Why did I feed their
disruptive power till all the
sands of this precious
never-to-be-repeated day
were shifted and stirred into
turmoil?
Jesus, I need the
balance of Your perspective.
Help me to magnify
only what's good and true.

Since all my days are Yours, Lord, even today belonged to You. (How often I wanted to say, "You can *have* it!")

The sun blazed through the window, prying my eyes open so very early. (However, I suppose it could have been raining.) And there stood my little boy with soggy pants and a cereal bowl. (Even so, he was smiling.)

The children dumped sticky oatmeal all over the shiny waxed floor. (At least we have enough to spill.) Phone calls and drop-in visits interrupted my day at every turn. (Yet You have blessed me with friends.)

There was fighting, teasing, and screaming the minute the schoolbooks hit the table. (Still, my boisterous children are normal and so healthy.) Then my little one pulled all the buds off the only plant I ever got to grow. (However, You will make it bloom again.)

Now they're all sweetly asleep, Lord, and it's so wonderfully quiet. (Why couldn't I remember all those "however" blessings while they were *awake*?)

For by the grace given me
I say to every one of you:
Do not think of yourself
more highly than you ought,
but rather think of yourself
with sober judgment,
in accordance with
the measure of faith
God has given you.
. . . Do not be conceited.

(Rom. 12:3, 16 NIV)

 **Self-Esteem**

Jesus,
teach me to
love myself
without a
megaphone.

Other women may not have this problem, but my mirror is positively unfriendly at six a.m. This morning I made the mistake of looking in that mirror without looking first in Jesus' face. As a result, I've been in trouble all day.

Over and over I've felt the need to prove that mirror wrong and re-establish my worth—to myself and others. Inadequacy has abrasively paraded as conceit. And no one was even watching—preoccupied as the world is with its own ego crises.

If I had spent time looking at and adoring God, I would have mirrored His love and moved beyond any need to impress. When I come to God, He accepts me with such completeness that I'm free to forget myself and concentrate on others.

It is only as I understand my worth in God's eyes that I can love myself in this healthy attitude of quiet humility and heart-felt gratitude. God measured my worth on the cross. There I cost Him the life of His only Son.

In the light of that cross I see self-acceptance as the responsibility to accept myself as God sees me—through Jesus Christ. I have absolutely no need for despair with such a God's-eye view. I certainly have no cause for pride, and positively no room for megaphones.

"I will praise the name of God, and will magnify Him with thanksgiving. . . . O magnify the Lord with me, and let us exalt His name together. . . . We love Him because he first loved us" (Pss. 69:30; 34:3; 1 John 4:19).

"Come unto me,
all ye that labor
and are heavy laden,
and I will give you rest."
(Matt. 11:28)

Moments of Quietness

The pastor prayed eloquently,
"Father, we thank You for
    moments of quietness."
Forgive my ignorance, Lord,
    but what and when is *quietness*?"

Oh, of course. It's the time the organ
    plays softly and people cough and
    babies fuss.
No? Then it's when I lock my bedroom
    door so the children's spats are muffled
    and distant.
No? It's probably when the dishwasher
    finally stops and the television
    blows a tube.
No? Maybe it's when I sleep and only
    the quiet noise of dreams scamper
    across my mind.
No again? Then it must be when I'm
    alone in the hills with only the chirp
    of birds and rustle of wind.

"No, My child, it's when you are alone
    with Me in the middle of life's
    raucous insanity."

Everyone faces days when the idea of running away from it all moves from the realm of distant dream to distinct desire.

Given the choice, who wouldn't swap jangling phones for a silent meadow of daisies, or bickering kids for a permanent seat at the symphony? Who wouldn't trade freeway fumes for cool salt air, or oceans of paperwork for rivers of hungry trout? Who would have trouble choosing between life's cramping frustration and open highways, or between conflicts and tranquil lagoons?

The trouble is, we're not often given such a choice. An even worse dilemma is to be given that choice and then find that there's no way to avoid taking oneself on the getaway.

It's a bad trip to discover my own lousy attitude can foul up fresh air anywhere. It's discouraging to detect that my insecurities and nagging guilt can muddy the water of even the most remote stream of escape.

It seems there's only one real route to escape. Next time I feel like running away from it all, Lord, remind me to run to You.

*"Lo, I am with you alway,
even unto the end
of the world."*
(Matt. 28:20)

Bridging the Gap

Jesus,
meet me on the bridge
between Sunday's
aspirations
and Monday's
exasperations.

Lustily I sang with the record album, " . . . and I will never walk alone, for Jesus walks beside me." I stopped abruptly. Maybe it's not really true. Maybe it's just some lovely ethereal thought.

Surely, Jesus, I silently pleaded, You haven't sorted Your way through the piles of unwashed clothes cluttering the bedroom or tripped over the toys in the hall. Could You have sat with me on the tub's edge cleaning tacky lemonade from the bottoms of Your feet, or gritted and ground Your way through that spilled sugar?

Did You walk with me to the medicine cabinet as I found a Dixie riddle cup and gulped a couple of aspirin for my headache? Were You beside me as I shoved aside newspapers and coloring books to collapse on the couch for a minute, only to be roused by screams from the children as the day's tenth civil war broke out?

I know. You were there through all of it. It's not that I think You can't take it, Lord. Obviously, anyone who endured Calvary isn't going to be overcome by the clutter and tumult of family life.

Perhaps I'm just embarrassed to realize You've been watching me sink beneath the pettiness of it all —especially since I made such high resolves to be a better mother after I heard that sermon on Sunday.

It would help if I'd remember You're not just observing, but offering help . . . that You're the rock above me, and still the Friend beside me.

I urge you to live a life
worthy of the calling
you have received
. . . and to put on the new self,
created to be like God
in true righteousness and holiness.
(Eph. 4:1, 24 NIV)

A Simple Statement

I know some, a few,
whose lives are a bold
exclamation point!
They drive hard in a slashing
downstroke toward a distant goal
no larger than a dot.
Yet somehow they never connect.

And I know some, too many,
whose searching lives
are a question mark.
I find them wandering,
curving and sloping
toward that elusive answer.
They, too, never reach the goal.

But there are others, too few,
whose lives are a
simple statement.
They do not reach for the truth,
they live in it.
They know Jesus. Period.

One of my dearest friends is a talented choral director and a very busy lady. She packs twenty pounds of living and serving into every five-pound day. Her time is spent so wisely and purposefully that there never seems to be time left over for complaining or self-centeredness. She has no time for saying, "It can't be done," or "Nobody ever did it that way before"; no time to make room for small thinking and pettiness; no time to worry that someone might not like her.

Yet she is liked—no, loved—because she knows the priority of a vital, growing relationship with God, and the importance of sharing His love through hugs, smiles, and an occasional encouraging wink. She saves moments for love, laughter, and appreciation . . . finds time to draw outsiders into her circle of warmth . . . time to do a job better than anyone thought it could be done . . . time to hear what's on your mind. And best of all, she spends a lifetime enthusiastically encouraging folks to be the best they can be for the Lord.

Once I slipped and fell in my walk up God's path. I was glad my friend called on the phone because I didn't want to look her in the eye. How easily she could have said, "I'm surprised," or "I'm disappointed." Instead she said, "I want you to know that I love you very much."

Not too long ago I sent her a card that said, "Knowing you has shown me so much of Him." That's a simple statement and a beautiful truth.

*Though I am
surrounded by troubles,
you will bring me
safely through them.*
(Ps. 138:7 LB)

Growing

It's hard to miss those
boulders of trouble
that roll into my life.
They're big enough
to climb on, so
I take Your hand, Jesus,
and scramble up with Your help.
It's those pebbles of
pressure,
noise,
and everyday frustration
that are nearly stoning
me senseless.
Lord, toughen my hide and
soften my heart.
Teach me to walk that slow
winding cobblestone path to
Christian maturity.

The morning greeted me with gray skies and a headache. The house was freezing. I shivered my way out to the kitchen to fix breakfast—no eggs, no juice, half a cup of milk. All three kids were at war, screaming, slugging, and tattling. My husband explained that I was to go to the store to buy a water pump for the broken washing machine sitting on stilts and leaking water in the middle of the kitchen. Then he left for work five minutes early without taking the kids to school. I shouldn't have blamed him—I wanted out too.

Our teenage daughter was hysterical because her hair wouldn't curl right. Our preschooler ran out the door in time to see Daddy's car rounding the corner and to throw himself screaming onto the sidewalk. I dressed to the tune of further hysterics from the bathroom. Daughter had tried cutting her hair in a panic and "would rather be bald than go to school like this!"

Next we had a search for the eight-year-old's lunch. Then he went off to school without his medication. The car stalled ten times as I tried to catch him with that medicine. When I finally reached the school, I was handed a pink paper by a teacher marching out front with a sign. The paper said, "Please tell your child he has crossed a picket line. We are on strike."

I went home wondering whether it would be legal for a mother to go on strike. Absentmindedly I began clearing debris. I tried to decide what to do with the load of dripping wash from the broken washer. I removed the milk carton from the sofa and decided to leave the tools on the dryer and the old water pump on the TV. Wearily, I sat down with a cup of coffee and said, "Maybe I'll write something. How much damage can I do with the typewriter, Lord?"—just as the return carriage knocked my coffee all over the table.

Suddenly I was laughing. Only God would have known to pile just one more thing on top of my morning of harassment. I hope I laugh sooner next time.

*"Be still and know
that I am God.
I am exalted
among the nations.
I am exalted in the earth!"*

(Ps. 46:10 RSV)

Circles

I'm whirling in
circles
like a child at play.
As You spin by me,
Lord,
remind my dizzied mind
that *I*
am the one who is
turning.

Standing alone in the dark solitude of the back yard, sipping hot chocolate and looking at the distant panorama of lights, I listened as the crickets sang with lusty, joyful abandon.

The sky was a blanket of blue-black with ridges of light clouds soaking up cast-off glow from an almost full moon—just dented a bit on one side.

I couldn't help looking at everything and saying as God did, "It is good." Only *my* voice had a touch of wonder in it, while *His* had only satisfaction.

So many days are spent chasing obligations in circles and nothing special seems to stand out as worth remembering. But five such unexpected minutes alone with God, just being still and truly seeing, truly appreciating, are worth a whole lifetime of chasing.

He himself bore our sins
in his body on the tree,
so that we might die to sins
and live for righteousness;
by his wounds
you have been healed.
(1 Peter 2:24 NIV)

God Available

Almighty God
who made the
delicate field daisy and
the limitless reaches of space,
who made the babe to suck
and the soul to search,
thank You for being
God Available.
No, more even than available.
Thank You for seeking me
first—for searching along
the agonizing road to
Golgotha,
then finding me blindly supplying
nails for Your Son's hands.
And when
I finally found
You, Lord,
Your bleeding hand was
reaching for mine.

I started to call for her and then found her in the kitchen kneeling on wrinkled old knees in a circle of scattered rice. I watched, fascinated, puzzled, as she picked up a single grain and took it to the sink, washed and dried it, then placed it in a bag.

After four or five grains had been salvaged, I asked, concerned, whether things were really so bad that she couldn't afford to sweep up the mess and buy a new bag of rice.

"Of course, dear," she said. "I was about to do just that when I suddenly had a thought and put away the broom. If I do it this way, maybe I can understand God a little better."

At my arching eyebrows, she hurried on. "What I thought was, in all of God's tremendous universe there is a tiny planet called earth. And on this earth exists a creation of God's called people. We people broke loose from the perfect pattern God had for us and turned against our Creator. We really made a terrible mess of things," she waved her hand at the floor. "And sometimes I wonder why God didn't just sweep up the mess and start all over. I really do wonder."

She shook her grayed head, then took another piece of rice to the sink and began thoughtfully rinsing it. "Instead, He went to amazing trouble and pain— even to the death of His only Son—to salvage the original bag of people."

Holding her freshly cleansed piece of rice to the light she said, ". . . and the blood of Jesus Christ his Son cleanseth us—*me*—from all sin!" (1 John 1:7). Then with shining eyes she placed the grain of rice gently in the bag as if it were worth all the world.

But our homeland
is in heaven,
where our Savior
the Lord Jesus Christ is.
(Phil. 3:20 LB)

Hints of Heaven

Someday, Lord,
I'll be fit to enjoy
heaven's beauty.
But for now,
thank You for making me
human enough
to think true beauty is
mounded clouds snuggling a
mountaintop,
water diving in a white frenzy
down a cliff,
palm fronds graciously
fanning Your skies,
delicate moss holding a rock
in its soft green clutch,
a child's cornsilk hair
flipping in the breeze,
fat baby fingers surveying
my face, and best of all,
that certain twinkle in
my husband's eyes.

Our three-year-old couldn't sleep. Creative thinking had conceived fear.

"Mommy, what will happen if the gas leaks and there's a big 'splosion?"

"There's no gas leaking, honey. Don't worry."

"Yes, it will. Then what will happen to me?"

"I'm sure it's not going to happen. But if it did, you would probably be hurt."

"And die?"

"Maybe. But, Matthew, don't worry. Jesus takes very good care of us. He's with us all the time—you just can't see Him."

"*He* might die in the 'splosion then!"

"No, honey. Jesus died once long ago—but He came back alive. And He'll never die again. He loves us *very* much. Anyway, Matt, when you die you get to go to heaven and see Jesus."

Great tears filled his eyes and voice. "Do I have to stay there? I want to come back home!"

My heart broke for him. Such frailty. Such need of me. Those fearful first steps of understanding what separation means. God, he's too young to call heaven his home.

Maybe I think I am, too.

Father, help me to set my feet, hands, and eyes on earthly things, but my heart on heavenly things. Today I need a touch of eternal perspective.

I will give to the LORD
the thanks due
his righteousness.
(Ps. 7:17 RSV)

Ceaseless Praise

Make my praise for You
rhythmic, Lord.
No more capricious spasms
of irregularity
or discontinuity.
Move my praise in an
upbeat tempo—
pulsating, lilting,
vibrating, even swinging,
yet never ceasing.
Show me that
Your righteousness is
alive with
rhythm and song.

It seems the bottom line on all our bills invariably reads, "Due and payable upon receipt." Who could miss it? We owe—they're collecting, and we had better pay up.

I wonder if God sends out such statements. I think He does. He tells me I owe Him my thanks, and it is due and payable now, not because my husband got a pay raise this year, not because the kids escaped the chicken pox, not even because God used me to bless someone's life.

I owe my Savior constant praise and thanks simply because of His righteousness—His nature that is completely fair and just—His personality that is total perfection and goodness.

This is good news. It means I can praise God when we don't get that pay raise, and when all three kids are scratching at chicken pox, making scars. Even when I totally blew my opportunity to be a blessing to someone, I am to praise God, because it's *Him* I'm to praise—not my circumstances, good or bad—and not my performance, good or bad.

This is good news. Instead of feeding God a stack of problems, complaints, and requests at prayer time, I can enjoy a celebration of His righteousness. God has required of me a joyful, praising heart and has given me a perfect, unchanging Target.

Therefore the LORD waits
to be gracious to you;
therefore he exalts himself
to show mercy to you.

(Isa. 30:18 RSV)

Waiting Line

I wait in long lines
wherever I go.
On the phone "please hold"
means ten minutes or so.
As I simmer at red lights,
my patience slow-leaks.
For appointments I'm told,
"We're booked solid for weeks."
Yet the God of my life
stands in wait for my call—
when I need an appointment
there is no wait at all.

I didn't want to be late for this particular doctor's appointment, because I'd had to wait nearly three months for it.

But traffic was uncooperative and every signal in town was out to detain me. Red used to be my favorite color.

The next two hours I spent in the doctor's waiting room, watching people shuffle in and out of the hallway leading to the inner cubicles. You know—those little rooms that you always enter without a magazine because you were naive enough to think you were going in to see the doctor; those rooms where you entertain yourself by deciphering impressive pharmaceutical words on a line-up of antiseptic bottles; or try to decide why they don't have cotton on *both* ends of their swabs; or calculate just how long it will take an industrial-strength air conditioner to freeze a human body clad in a flimsy paper gown.

When at last my name was called and the doctor finally came, he bustled in all smiles and apologies for the little emergency that had him running a "bit" late. And I found myself saying, "Oh, that's O.K., no problem. Did you know that the squares on your ceiling have one hundred and ninety-four holes each? Except for that row over there at the edge. You can see that those had to be trimmed so they only have one hundred and *twenty-six* holes. . . ."

"Say 'ah,' please."

I doubt that doctors really need people to say "ah" in order to see their throats. It might just be a good substitute for the sounds most people make when they're weary with waiting for the attention of a busy and important person.

It's hard to believe that the most important One in the universe is constantly available. I wonder if I tend to keep *Him* waiting just because I'm so used to having Him on call twenty-four hours a day?

*"Does he not
see my ways
and count my every step?"*

(Job 31:4 NIV)

Moving Day

Here I stand, Lord,
waiting for the holy elevator
that will lift me swiftly, easily
to Christian maturity.
Make me content to take
one small growing step
after another,
climbing the stairs with You.

Apparently my celestial staircase was not built by the same construction crew that does cathedrals. In fact, I suspect it was thrown together by the crew that erects circus tents, whose motto is: Just as long as it hangs together till the show's over.

Today, for example, I climbed through a lot of clutter.

It was midnight when I finally got as far as the dirty dishes. They couldn't be done sooner because the peaches were rotting and it was either make haste and make jam, or make waste.

And the kids had been so bad all day, it would have saved time to set the alarm at ten-minute intervals for a lecture, a spanking, or a mop-up.

And the washing simply had to be done that day since our daughter had returned from camp with a duffel bag of sopping clothes that were mildewing and required an accompanying nose-clip. Evidently they were caught in a downpour that nearly washed their tent away.

And there was the medicine I needed to pick up for the little one who had tonsilitis (again), but there was no one to watch the children until Daddy got home . . . and he was three hours late, since they'd had another of their ritual emergencies at work.

And all this had to be worked in between phone calls from people wanting me to watch their kids for a little while, or work on a committee, or bake something, since I "don't work" and am home all day— probably reading novels, watching soap operas, and painting my toenails!

It's difficult to remember that even on days like this, when my stairs are carpeted with problems, they're leading just as surely to heaven. As long as I keep climbing, keep laughing at myself, and keep looking up.

The LORD delighteth in thee.
(Isa. 62:4)

Delight thyself also
in the LORD;
and he shall give thee
the desires of thine heart.
(Ps. 37:4)

Delight Full

I know You said it, Lord,
but I'm having trouble imagining
You delighting in me.
Patience and mercy
I can believe.
But delight?
You know that with me You get
intentions as often as accomplishment—
letdown as often as love.
Delight?
In me?

Yes, child, I said it.
I delight not in your
excellence, but in your need of
Mine.
Delight!
In Me!

Now there's a command I can obey, Lord. How easy it is to enjoy You. As natural as a small child savoring a world that surprises with snowflakes on the nose; seeds floating on gossamer wings; tree branches that hold birds' nests, dancing leaves, and sweet fruit.

I delight—in Your love that reaches right through my walls of unworthiness; in Your holy perfection that causes my spirit to dance in worship; in Your power that somehow longs to be spent through me; in Your absolute worthiness that commands not only my delight, but my life.

Yes, Lord, I do delight in You. And You knew how it would turn out. I find that the desire of my heart is only for more of You.

How lovely that You arranged it so I would ask for the best Gift of all.

*"Have you an arm
like God . . . ?"*

(Job 40:9 RSV)

*Neither did their own arm save them;
but thy right hand and thine arm,
and the light of thy countenance,
because thou hadst
a favour unto them.*

(Ps. 44:3)

 Ouch!

Father,
why do I
strain my frail
wrists
when You offer Your
mighty arm?

It wasn't until my Datsun was trapped between the curb and the bumper of the car in front of me that I knew I'd been right. The parking space was too small.

Only one, positively no more than two miserable inches of space to maneuver that stubborn steering wheel—one exhausting inch forward, one weary inch back. Leaning back on the seat, I groaned at our decision that power steering was a luxury we didn't need.

It was then that he came, lightly touching the edge of his cowboy hat—a stranger with a smile, biceps, and a simple offer, "Let me help."

The smile had traces of amusement, mixed with sympathy. I didn't care. I quickly climbed out, relinquishing the driver's seat to this strong, capable solution. Let him wrestle with my predicament. He was better equipped to handle it.

Folding his six-foot frame into the small seat, he restarted the engine and in one stroke backed neatly alongside the curb. Openmouthed with disbelief, I could only think, "Well, I *knew* I almost had it!"

Maybe, Lord, I'm always so tired because I lose my strength in the driver's seat struggling to extricate myself from my own traps. Then I lose the joy, finally turning it over to You, but saying as You solve it, "I knew I almost had it!"

Blessed be the LORD!
For he has heard
the voice of my supplications.
The LORD is my strength and my shield;
in him my heart trusts;
so I am helped,
and my heart exults,
and with my song I give thanks to him.
The LORD is the strength
of his people.

(Ps. 28:6–8 RSV)

The Gift of Strength

Lord,
You tell me Your strength is a gift.
I'll accept that.
But I find myself holding out for
one huge package, wrapped, ribboned,
and presented with fanfare.
What did I do with all those simple
now-sized packages You
presented daily at
just the right time,
in just the right amount?
Is Your strength like manna—
plenty for now
but not to be stored?

I'm feeling weak today, Father, and totally inadequate for the climb before me. This job looms like a mountain. And I feel as though I'm climbing it, weighted down with an enormous backpack bulging with—what? Heavy responsibilities? The burden of my potential?

I've been struggling under the weight—scrambling over boulders, sliding on loose rock with frayed slippery-soled tennis shoes, clutching at projections with bare and bleeding hands.

But this morning, when I finally stopped long enough to rest and lay my burden at Your feet, You opened that backpack for me. I was surprised to see it had a bow on it. Only presents have bows.

You showed me pitons and ropes, axes and hammers, and genuine climbing boots and gloves. I feel so silly, Lord. Here I've been lugging on my back all the gear You provided for climbing.

Teach me to use all this equipment so that I can follow You all the way to the windy summit if necessary. I don't like heights, but I'll follow. Because I know and love the One who is leading, more than I know and love my insecurities.

Dear children,
let us not love
with words or tongue
but with actions and in truth.

(1 John 3:18 NIV)

Learning Love

God,
help me to love You
the way You
deserve
to be loved—
with doing,
not dreaming;
with obedience,
not oratories;
on my feet,
not just my knees.

It's hard to say how many people could look at a picture of an old metal sprinkling can with corks plugging some, but never quite all the holes in its leaking sides and say, "That's me!" *I* said it.

The picture was on the front of a card my sister had sent me. "Never," I muttered to myself, "have I seen such a graphic picture of what keeps happening to my schedule. People just keep shooting it full of holes—and they're shooting faster than I can stop them."

I opened the card and read, "Keep plugging! Love you!" What a dear sister I have. And how reassuring to be loved with such appropriate understanding.

Then I noticed a postscript on the card. She had managed to turn her love into an action verb by adding, "Can I help you have some free time to write by borrowing your two handsome boys for a while?"

My sister definitely does not have time to love this actively. She has four active little children of her own, plus several more that she babysits. And since they live over a hundred miles away, when she gets our boys, it's for days—not hours.

Yet somewhere she must have learned the importance of loving not just in word, but in deed.

I'm trying to think of the last time I added a practical P.S. to my declarations of love to God. . . .

*They will go to church,
yes, but they won't really
believe anything they hear.*
(2 Tim. 3:5 LB)

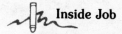 **Inside Job**

The church was closed down,
no worship afforded.
Hearts were nailed shut
before windows were boarded.

The sermon was vital, but really, it was dragging on a bit. Beside me a rotund man dropped his chins lower and lower, dozing deeply. Could I be hearing right—was he actually snoring?

He was.

In the silence of my mind I gingerly suggested, *It's Your house, Lord. Why don't You poke him?* and then watched.

His leg began to move and his thumbs jerked, like a horse twitching at bothersome flies.

He slept on.

How could a person insult God by sleeping through a worship service? I fumed. *I wouldn't even consider napping in church!*

Yet I had to wonder—do I excuse myself for drowsing through life? At times have I squirmed and shrugged, yet slumbered on, ignoring God's probing finger that called me to wake to urgent needs around me?

I wonder which is worse. Those who openly sleep? Or those who sing hymns and smile and tip God in the offering plate, but are hibernating spiritually?

For you were called
to freedom, brethren;
only do not use your freedom
as an opportunity for the flesh,
but through love
be servants of one another.

(Gal. 5:13 RSV)

Boundaries

God, look at me!
Confined to pages flipped on the calendar,
stuck in a wear-dated body,
trapped in a tongue-tied heart,
bound on the ropes of repetition,
perimetered by fences of frustration,
caught thrashing in the net of humanity.
Oh, limitless Lord!
Give me wings to soar above the
    boundaries,
free in the boundless arms of Your love.

The morning had been fairly routine—until I discovered the bird trapped in the family room. Someone had left the screen door open a mere sparrow's-width, so one had hopped in.

Perched quivering on the arm of the couch, the pathetic little bird splattered pale droplets of fear on the upholstery. At my startled sound, he took flight, crashing first into one window and then another. Finally, exhausted, he clutched a ledge for a brief and trembling rest before trying to break free again.

Soothingly, I spoke to him, "No, little bird, not that way. That clearly appears to be the way out, but you'll only break your neck. This way, see?" I offered, sliding the screen door wide open.

It's impossible to communicate with birds. I found I can't chirp their language, and my "soothing" voice only drove him back to bashing his beak against the invisible barrier that separated him from that blue sky.

So I hid and watched with silent frustration. He simply couldn't find the open door. Every time he saw white clouds through that window, he went once more for sure destruction.

Then a surprising thing happened. From outside, another sparrow hopped toward the open door. He moved right up to the doorjamb, loudly chirping the way to freedom. And it worked.

As his trapped friend paused, he heard and cocked his feathered head, riveting his attention to the liberating call. He jumped from the couch arm, to the cushion, to the floor. He listened, not yet seeing, but following the call closer and closer. Then one more hop and he was out with his friend, flying free.

Sometimes I feel trapped. Sometimes I bash my head into life's unyielding windowpanes. It's those times I need to be reminded that You, Lord, are the only Way out. Thank You for brothers and sisters who care enough to sound the call to freedom in Christ.

Again Jesus said,
". . . Do you truly love me?"
(John 21:16 NIV)

Exercise in Love

The best exercise for
strengthening our
relationship to God is
deep knee bends.
But why not in
a field of daisies?

There's always someone who'll say it. Solemn with the weight of untold anniversaries, he nods and says, "Yes indeed. A good marriage doesn't just happen—it takes real *work*." He thereby places the maintenance of a healthy marriage in a category with push-ups in the army.

Marriage does require constant attention. And even the smoothest ones have an occasional rough spot. But if marriage is supposed to be work, I'd better start being nervous. Any minute somebody's going to catch me playing on the job, because when you really love someone, spending time with that person could be defined almost any way *except* work.

It's not drudgery, but a creative, exhilarating, and satisfying exercise in love. It's not boring callisthenics, but a lively game of tennis or a jog through the woods in springtime.

After more than nineteen years of marriage, I have not yet found myself saying, "Now I'm just going to have to *make* some time to sit down with my husband this evening and let him share what's on his mind." Those quiet times of sharing are cherished and anticipated. They're my dessert for a ten-course day.

God's Word tells us we are the Bride of Christ. Perhaps we can measure the health of that relationship by asking, "Do I spend time with Jesus from *eagerness,* or *obligation?*"

He heals the brokenhearted,
and binds up their wounds.
(Ps. 147:3 RSV)

Repair Work

When a fractured leg is healed
it must walk again;
when a damaged zipper is mended
it must zip again;
when a sagging gate is fixed
it must swing again;
and when a broken heart is mended
it must give again.

He came to me, large eyes wet with hurt and bewilderment. His hand, not quite four years old, curved beneath the cold stiffness of his beloved hamster. "Mommy! Jeff says Sammy's *dead*." A tear slipped, splashing on the soft white fur. "He won't wake up. See?" His finger gently poked at the unyielding side.

"Oh, honey, he *is* dead. I'm sorry."

"Why, Mommy? *Why* won't he move?"

"That's what 'dead' is, sweetheart. It means things don't move or breathe any more. It means Sammy *can't* wake up. You see, he's not sleeping—he's dead."

He had asked "why"—why is there death? I had answered "what," giving a coldly accurate description of death. How can I explain the why of death when I don't understand it myself? Oh, I know that death is in the world because of sin. But why does a little boy's pet hamster have to die?

And why did our newborn baby have to die? All I could do was trust God for the reasons. I hoped in Him and leaned on Him. Still, that's not truly understanding. The cold fact is: death separates. And death hurts.

How much more it must hurt those who don't have God to lean on, those who have no hope of eternal life in Christ Jesus.

I remember crying out, when the wounds of death were fresh and throbbing and my arms were awkward with their emptiness, "Dear God, what do I do with empty arms?"

Perhaps now I know, now that the wounds are healed.

Empty arms can reach out and hug hope into empty souls. Empty arms can embrace a sorrowing world that needs to meet its Savior.

Casting all your care
upon him;
for he careth for you.
(1 Peter 5:7)

Casting on Christ

Lord,
how many times have I
gone fishing for Your help
with my pole of prayer?
I brace myself on the
edge of a sea of trouble and
with practiced style
cast my cares on You—
then skillfully
reel them in.
Over and over.
Maybe when my cares become
too heavy to
tie on the end of a line,
I'll finally lay aside
the rod and cast
myself
on You—
with no strings attached.

Our pastor had just implied that worry might be a sin. Then he leaned into the pulpit and said, "Will all those who ever worry please remain seated."

What an unfair approach! I was forced to remain seated and be labeled a "worrier," because if I stood, I was worried I'd be the only one. Plus, I felt a twinge of anxiety that someone might think I wasn't being completely honest if I got to my feet.

Being a very forward-thinking man, our pastor then taught us to worry scientifically. Evidently, statistics have proven that over 80 percent of what we fret about never happens. So we waste a lot of valuable time.

To conserve this wasted time he suggested we make a weekly "worry list," jotting down all our concerns as they occur. However, we are not permitted to stew about these things until a designated time—say at three o'clock Thursday afternoon, if that's convenient.

If someone should happen to drop by and ask what we're doing, we're to say, "Can't you see? I'm worrying. I'm on number sixteen. I'll be through in a few minutes."

Really, this is no joking matter. Some people struggle openly with this thorny problem. Worse, there are others who are well-established worriers and don't even seem to know it. I worry about these people most.

It's imperative that we recognize our propensity to label worry as "godly concern" and legitimize it as a recurring "prayer request." It's crucial that we acknowledge God's loving care and ability to handle these concerns. But it's most essential that we learn the freedom of casting all our cares on Christ, who is able to keep to the uttermost that which we *truly* commit to Him.

Then . . . he said to them,
"Come with me by yourselves
to a quiet place
and get some rest."

(Mark 6:31 NIV)

Hug-Hungry

Often my hungry arms
ache
for a squeeze of my
little one.
But he's
digging tunnels,
tossing balls,
or running in the wind.
Much too busy for hugs.
Dear heavenly Father,
I seem so busy too.
Do Your arms ever
ache for me?

What's going on this morning, Lord? I have work to do. But the sun is coaxing me with bright promises and the day is blooming ripe with succulent choices.

It seems that even my household chores have turned on me, conspiring to tempt me with visions of escape. Rumpled sheets on unmade beds teasingly imitate tossing, swirling waves. Mounds of soiled clothes piled beside the washing machine emulate rolling hills waiting to be explored.

The shaggy green carpet, unvacuumed, slyly suggests a sweeping lawn of vibrant grass, offering a spongy cool treat to feet imprisoned in leather.

I'm weakening, Lord! All this work will be here tomorrow—but will the sun? Is wisdom sometimes found in following the heart to refreshment—in following the soul to You?

Maybe we should discuss this further with damp grass between my toes, Lord.

Maybe I need to rest in Your arms. . . .

I wish I might be present
with you right now
and try a new way
of speaking.
(Gal. 4:20 MLB)

Now

Lord,
give me the sense to
love,
appreciate,
and spend precious time
with my children
now
so that someday
I won't feel the need to
smother my grandchildren
with attention
that belonged to
their parents.

One of my mother's delightful ideas is to write birthday letters to all six of her grown children. These messages warmly and lovingly assure us that we have, indeed, turned out all right.

My letter came today. Either it's terribly late for my last birthday, or a few months early for the next one—I'm not sure which. In either case I'm thrilled, because she said she was glad I arrived—glad I was born into her family, and doubly pleased that I was born again into God's family.

Musing on my childhood, she recalled that there was never really any friction between us except in my tendency to be in a "dream world." She claimed I still have some of that in my make-up, but she now realizes this is the "creative part" of me.

Imagine that! Just because I occasionally don't hear my kids talking to me when they're two urgent inches in front of my face, she says I'm in a dream world! She wrote:

I'm sure that you continue to find this creates problems and conflicts as you try to balance the practical everyday world with the ideas and dreams in your head and heart.

There are car pools, children's problems, husband's needs, minor and major crises, routine chores, etc. Your ideas are circling around, putting meanings to all these things and your husband and kids are saying, "Look at me!"

It's a big job, isn't it? Putting practical on one side of the scale and just the right amount of creativity on the other to make a good balance.

Our time doesn't always have to be divided equally, but our attention needs to be concentrated wholly on one or the other during each encounter!

Amen to that bit of insight. All we have is now. And the now-moments with our children are as brief as a baby's first smile, as irretrievable as a missed hug.

Not by might,
nor by power,
but by my Spirit,
says the LORD of hosts.

(Zech. 4:6 RSV)

High Expectations

God expects
more than our best—
He expects
His best through us.

It was only ten minutes until the worship service was to begin, and there was low-key panic in the choir room. We had been working hard, but the morning's anthem was a rough number. We were making it sound even rougher.

Of about seventy choir members that day, only two were tenors. The basses were lost somewhere in the first four measures, and the sopranos were so flat that I kept looking to see if they'd been leveled by a steam roller. We altos weren't so sure of our notes either, and our entrances and exits may as well have been unmarked intersections.

Our director wasn't wasting time telling us how we sounded, but was rehearsing us in a frantic double-time tempo—not even seeming to breathe between shouted commands. We all knew, though. We'd have had to be deaf not to know.

The last minute before we went in to face that poor unsuspecting congregation, our director closed her eyes and said, "Lord, we've done our best, and we need some help from You. Send Your angels to sing with us. We do this for Your glory." Then she told us to relax and enjoy praising God.

As we sang, it was all I could do not to crane my head to look down the rows of blue robes to see where those angels were standing. The expressions on the face of pastor and people mirrored our marvel. And they didn't even know that minutes before, our beautiful song of praise had been in musical disarray.

We may feel at times that God expects more than we can give. But if we ask, He gives more than we could ever expect. We are privileged to give it back to Him in praise and service.

Who can discern his errors?
Forgive my hidden faults.
Keep your servant also from willful sins;
may they not rule over me.
Then I will be blameless,
innocent of great transgression.
May the words of my mouth
and the meditation of my heart
be pleasing in your sight,
O LORD, my Rock and my Redeemer.

(Ps. 19:12–14 NIV)

Self-Protection

Protect me, Lord!
I don't mean just from
danger without,
but from danger within.

Protect me from
the folded pages of
self-deception,
the rounded corners of
convenience,
the glossy surface of
rationalization,
the wide margins of
broadmindedness.

Protect me from
being pressed between the
pages of my own
willful ways.

Through my windshield I could see that it was one of those fickle days when surly gray clouds dare to mingle with the gentle whites amid startling patches of blue.

My highway concentration was interrupted by my young son's voice from the back seat. "Mom, the sun and clouds are taking turns." And I agreed with a laugh, as I removed my sunglasses once more in rhythm with the sun's recession.

But I knew—of course I really knew—that in God's nature the sun never recedes. That brilliant ball of fire never takes turns with anything. And the blue heaven is ever back there somewhere.

It's only the clouds that obscure—in nature, and in men's souls. Black stormy clouds of trouble and sin, and white puffy clouds of selfish ease and lax attitudes come between us and the Son.

How prone we are to wander in the heavy haze of self-deception that dampens God's unalterable truths and waters down their impact on our lives.

Oh, for the wind of God's loving breath that scuttles clouds and haze before it, leaving clear the brilliant blue promise of hope in Christ.

*The things
which are impossible with men
are possible with God.*
(Luke 18:27)

Behold, I make all things new.
(Rev. 21:5)

Change Me

Lord,
make of my hostility
hospitality,
of my brokenness
beauty,
of my pain
praise,
of myself a
servant.

It was lesson time, and father and son were hunched over a third-grade math book.

"See if you can answer this one," I heard my husband saying. Was there a slight twinkle of playfulness in his voice? "Pretend I give you nine oranges and two eggs. How many do you have?"

Smugly and without hesitation, the answer came. "Eleven. That was easy. Math's my best subject, you know."

"Eleven *what,* son?" The amusement was full blown now—Daddy had him trapped. He was about to demonstrate that you can't mix oranges and eggs.

I stepped into the study to watch the expression on my son's face. Pausing, with mouth open and brows thoughtfully drawn together, he said, "Orange Julius drinks, I guess!"

The expression worth watching was on my husband's face, and on mine too. Had our son missed the point, or made it?

There are days I am expected to mix patience with problems and come up with peace. The equation doesn't always compute. I need to remember who the Miracle-Worker is.

Lord, help me learn to hand You life's unmixables, then watch You add them up to something creative—something new, something called a miracle.

*No greater joy
can I have than this,
to hear that my children
follow the truth.*

(3 John 4)

My Boy

I look at the shiny-shaggy hair
and round, blue-gray eyes;
the small pink tongue struggling
impatiently against tiny white teeth
to form a word,
to convey an exciting new-born thought;
the broad little boy hand
covered with dirt, reaching
to touch my cheek;
and suddenly I realize
the astounding responsibilities
that are mine before that hand
expands to a man's hand.
O God,
hold my son's hand while he crosses
the danger-filled street to manhood.

This was to be my stay-at-home-and-get-a-few-things-done day. That would be just fine, except for one thing: I have a toddler who wants to help.

I finish the washing, and he struggles the piles of clean clothes toward their dresser drawers. I suppose a hundred years from now I won't care that they started the trip neatly folded.

I sweep the floor, and he insists on helping me by emptying the dustpan. In the overall scheme of things, I suppose the fact that he dumped the dirt back onto the floor is relatively unimportant.

I begin mixing ingredients for yeast rolls, and he insists on adding the flour. If I look at the situation optimistically, unbleached white is a good color on me.

I do know he's really trying, Lord. And I know he needs practice to learn. But it would truly be so much easier to simply do it myself.

I watch, filled with apprehension, as he teeters toward me, chubby hands cupping fragile eggs, and I'm suddenly aware that You, God, have entrusted me with the fragile life of this child. Guide me as I help my little helper become Your man.

Live life . . . with a due sense
of responsibility,
not as men [and women]
who do not know the meaning
and purpose of life
but as those who do.
Make the best use
of your time,
despite all the difficulties
of these days.

(Eph. 5:15–16 PHILLIPS)

Timely Appreciation

Jesus, please
teach me to appreciate
what I have
before time
forces me to appreciate
what I had.

Someone asked me what I'd change about my life if I could. I didn't like the question, because without pausing, my mind took one giant and well-traveled leap backward to the church and the dear friends we'd left behind in the last year. My imagination nestled comfortably into the familiar memory of warm hugs, special times of sharing and prayer, and the relaxing comfort of knowing and being known.

I squirmed with the realization that I was being forced to choose between the past and the present. I knew better. The past is never a viable choice.

Yet *had* I been stiff-arming the present in favor of warm memories? Was I building walls to insulate against future pain? After all, the relationships of today could become the losses of tomorrow. And just so, I realized, the lost moments of today would become the empty memories of tomorrow.

With God's help, I will not sacrifice any more precious clusters of days, or even minutes, to the fire of regret or the consuming backward look. For it is corporally impossible to look backward and forward at the same time. And Jesus is always forward, calling us to keep pace with Him.

The Lord, your Redeemer
who made you, says,
All things were made by me;
I alone stretched out the heavens.
By myself I made the earth
and everything in it.

(Isa. 44:24 LB)

Hands Off

When I come to God
with all my questions,
requests, and yes,
sometimes suggestions,
I forget with all these
needs so pressing
just who it is
I am addressing.
If God is God
He can act in love
with just my praise
and not my shove.
At last I see,
my heart understands,
why I'm taught to pray
with folded hands.

My first clue that I'd been dangerously relegating God to the level of dusty sandals and flapping robes came this morning. I found myself handing Him a list of possible solutions along with my prayer requests.

Perhaps He doesn't need my help. I just remembered that all by Himself, without any assistance from me, He formed the worlds.

Scooping endless reaches of space, He molded flaming balls of fire and hurled their shining light to the darkest corners. He shaped earthen globes and set them spinning about those fiery suns. Some He splashed with water and life.

He mounded dark hills, sprinkled their tops with powdered snow, and accented them with valleys of green—covered with graceful trees, gentle streams, and scampering wildlife.

Reaching down, He punctuated the green with flowers of crimson, gold, purple, and white; then He set them all dancing with the sweet wind of His breath and sparkling with the light of His smile.

Forgive me, God, for trying to force You into cartons sized to my notions, needs, and desires. You cannot be boxed in. Forgive me for the ignorance of trying to mold You. Perfection is unbendable.

Mold *me,* Lord. Shape my mouth to fit Your praise, my feet to fit Your paths, my hands to fit Your tasks, my desires to fit Your will, and my understanding to fit the reality of You.

*My voice shalt thou hear
in the morning, O L*ORD*:
in the morning will I
direct my prayer unto thee
and will look up.*

(Ps. 5:3)

*But lay up for yourselves
treasure in heaven
where neither moth
nor rust doth corrupt,
and where thieves
do not break through nor steal.*

(Matt. 6:20)

Tithing Time

Your Word says,
Give Me of your first fruits,
that which is new and fresh,
that which you'd like to keep.

Does that mean I must give You
the first hour of my day, Lord,
that choice hour for sleeping
or waking slowly?
Do You already claim that hour
for Yourself?
Have I been robbing You?

"You've been robbing
yourself, child."

The news wasn't that noteworthy, even though we were watching the channel that continually sings its own praises, claiming lively and thorough coverage of the day's events. So I didn't really mind the interruption when it came. In fact, I welcomed it.

Our youngest son had plopped himself in my lap, slipped his arms around my neck, and then pressed his nose against mine. No chance of watching the news now—all I could see were eyeballs and eyelashes. He always has known how to capture my complete attention.

"Mommy," he whispered. "Could you get me that shiny bike we saw today? You know, the red one."

"No, honey," I whispered back, going slightly cross-eyed with our close-range conference. "I'm sorry, but it costs too much money."

"Just write a check," he recommended.

Ah! So he had discovered checks without discovering their principle. He didn't understand that we cannot withdraw what we did not deposit.

I do understand, but sometimes I forget that truth. When I try to make a withdrawal, needing reserves of love and patience, I occasionally find my heavenly account bankrupt. On such days it seems I'm trying to cash in to get the goods, when I've failed to set aside the riches of time spent with God and His Word.

No wonder Jesus said we are to lay up for ourselves treasures in heaven.

I'm glad He's open for deposits around the clock. I suspect He may have noticed . . . I didn't get my "banking" done this morning.

*And our prayer
is for your perfection.*
(2 Cor. 13:9 NIV)

*"Be perfect, therefore,
as your heavenly Father
is perfect."*
(Matt. 5:48 NIV)

Permanent Solution

My hair just won't hold a curl.
Every day it needs reset.
I guess I need a permanent.

That's just like my goodness.
It doesn't last either.
Every day I run to You, Lord,
for more of Your goodness.

Do You give permanents?
Oh!
Eternity is a permanent.

It had become necessary to explain to my indignant preteen the difference between being perfect and being a mother. My explanation left much room for discussion.

As a very young boy he probably did think Mommy was perfect. Now that, in his maturity, he no longer lives under such a delusion, he's taken it upon himself to firmly yank the rug out from under any false pretenses I might be standing on. "You think you're perfect, so we always have to do what you say. Well you're not perfect!"

Bad enough to have to hear news like this—but from one so young! How soon today's children drop the blanket of innocence.

Actually, my son had simply and predictably ceased to equate authority with faultlessness. So it was time to explain perfection.

Perfect means without flaw. Perfect says, "no change needed." Perfect doesn't grow, because there's no place to go. Perfect just *is*. Perfect isn't a word. It's a name: God's.

Someday we will be perfect in Christ Jesus. In the meantime, we are in the process of being *made* perfect (Col. 1:28).

Perhaps our children are in the process of being made perfect through patience with us (James 1:4).